MW01131114

COUNTRY PROFILES

NORWAY

BY CHRIS BOWMAN

BELLWETHER MEDIA • MINNEAPOLIS, MN

Blastoff! Discovery launches a new mission: reading to learn. Filled with facts and features, each book offers you an exciting new world to explore!

This edition first published in 2020 by Bellwether Media, Inc.

No part of this publication may be reproduced in whole or in part without written permission of the publisher.
For information regarding permission, write to Bellwether Media, Inc., Attention: Permissions Department,
6012 Blue Circle Drive, Minnetonka, MN 55343.

Library of Congress Cataloging-in-Publication Data

Names: Bowman, Chris, 1990- author.
Title: Norway / by Chris Bowman.
Description: Minneapolis, MN : Bellwether Media, Inc., 2020. |
    Series: Blastoff! Discovery: Country Profiles | Includes
    bibliographical references and index. | Audience: Ages 7-13. |
    Audience: Grades 3-8. | Summary: "Engaging images accompany
    information about Norway. The combination of high-interest subject
    matter and narrative text is intended for students in grades 3
    through 8"– Provided by publisher.
Identifiers: LCCN 2019037209 (print) | LCCN 2019037210 (ebook)
    | ISBN 9781644871713 (library binding) | ISBN
    9781618918475 (ebook)
Subjects: LCSH: Norway–Juvenile literature. | Norway–Social life and
    customs–Juvenile literature.
Classification: LCC DL409 .B69 2020 (print) | LCC DL409 (ebook)
    | DDC 948.1–dc23
LC record available at https://lccn.loc.gov/2019037209
LC ebook record available at https://lccn.loc.gov/2019037210

Text copyright © 2020 by Bellwether Media, Inc. BLASTOFF!
DISCOVERY and associated logos are trademarks
and/or registered trademarks of Bellwether Media, Inc.

Editor: Rebecca Sabelko   Designer: Brittany McIntosh

Printed in the United States of America, North Mankato, MN.

TABLE OF CONTENTS

Brightly painted buildings greet a family visiting Bergen. They begin their day by walking to *bryggen*, or "the dock," which is the oldest part of the city. The family admires the wooden buildings painted red, yellow, and white. They explore the narrow alleys and stop by the shops and cafes.

OTHER TOP SITES

BERGEN

GEIRANGERFJORD

JOTUNHEIMEN NATIONAL PARK

KJERAG

OSLO OPERA HOUSE

After stopping by the fish market for a snack, the family walks to the *Fløibanen*. They ride this **funicular** rail line up Mount Fløyen. They stop for a moment to take in the view of the city. It has been a great morning in one of Norway's most beautiful cities!

BARENTS
SEA

JAN MAYAN

SVALBARD

NORWEGIAN
SEA

ARCTIC CIRCLE

TRONDHEIM

NORWAY

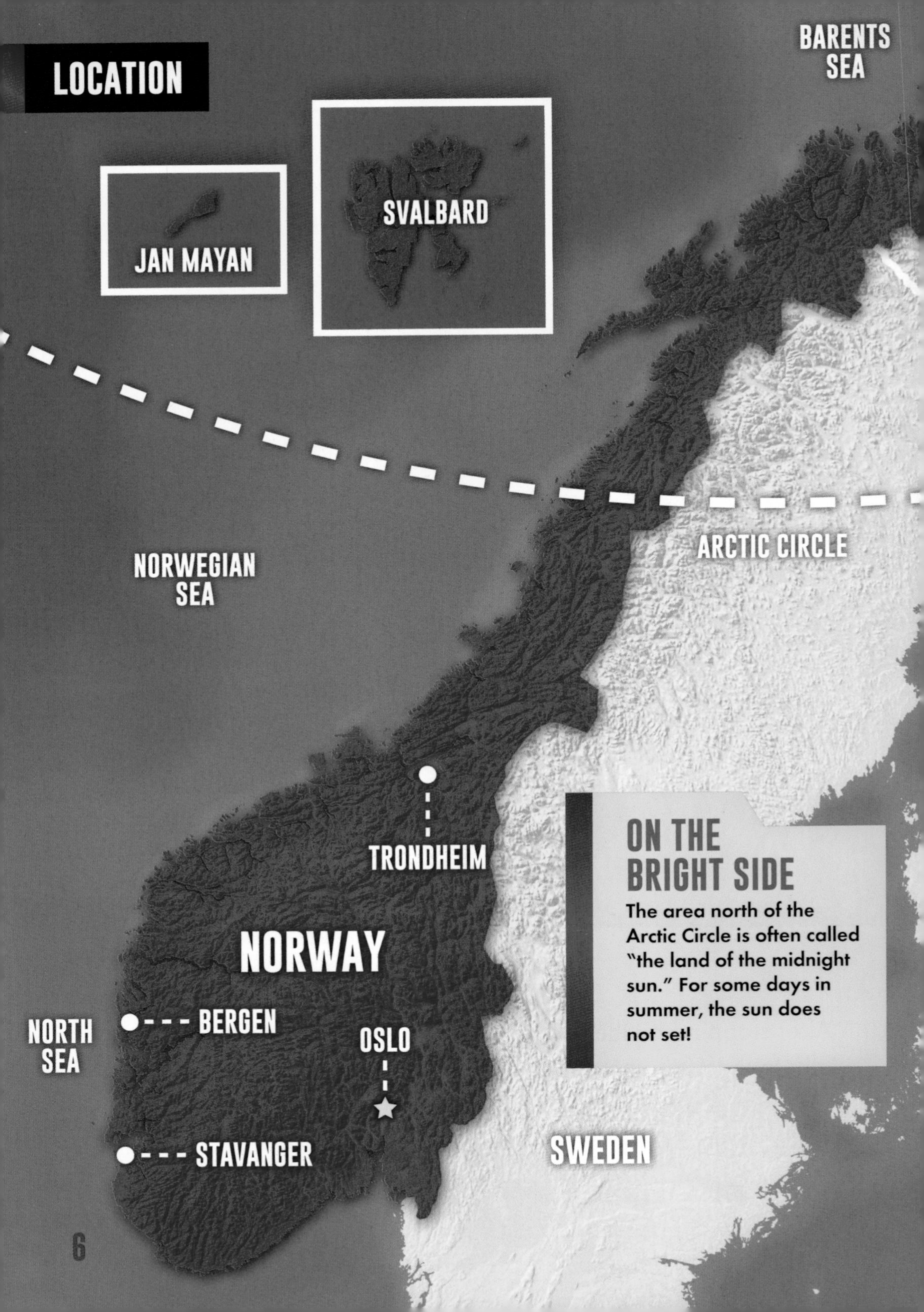

ON THE
BRIGHT SIDE

The area north of the
Arctic Circle is often called
"the land of the midnight
sun." For some days in
summer, the sun does
not set!

NORTH
SEA

BERGEN

OSLO

STAVANGER

SWEDEN

RUSSIA

FINLAND

Norway is a long, thin country that covers 125,021 square miles (323,802 square kilometers). It also includes the islands of Svalbard and Jan Mayen. Oslo, the capital city, rests in the nation's southeastern corner. Norway is one of three countries on the northern European **peninsula** called **Scandinavia**. The top third of **mainland** Norway is above the **Arctic Circle**.

The seas of the Atlantic and Arctic Oceans shape much of Norway's borders. The North Sea washes along the southern coast. The Norwegian Sea is to the west. The frigid waters of the Barents Sea form the country's northern border. Russia, Finland, and Sweden neighbor Norway to the east.

N
W + E
S

LANDSCAPE AND CLIMATE

Much of Norway's landscape is made up of **plateaus** and the Scandinavian Mountains. Many of these are covered by snow or **glaciers**, including the northernmost Finnmark Plateau. The rough **terrain** is also dotted with lakes and scarred by deep river valleys. The land becomes gentle rolling hills in the southeast. Norway's rocky western coast is lined with islands and many famously large **fjords**, such as Sognefjord.

= SCANDINAVIAN MOUNTAINS
= FINNMARK PLATEAU

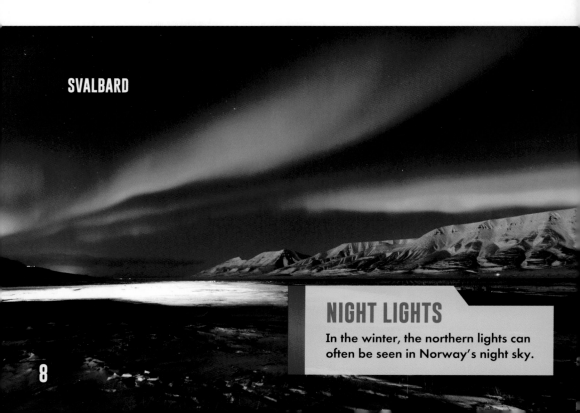

SVALBARD

NIGHT LIGHTS

In the winter, the northern lights can often be seen in Norway's night sky.

SOGNEFJORD

OSLO

Average seasonal highs and lows

JANUARY
HIGH: 29 °F (-2 °C)
LOW: 20 °F (-7 °C)

APRIL
HIGH: 48 °F (9 °C)
LOW: 33 °F (1 °C)

JULY
HIGH: 71 °F (22 °C)
LOW: 54 °F (12 °C)

OCTOBER
HIGH: 49 °F (9 °C)
LOW: 39 °F (4 °C)

°F = degrees Fahrenheit
°C = degrees Celsius

Norway has a warmer climate than many other northern countries. The warm currents of the **Gulf Stream** bring mild temperatures north. It is often rainy near the coast.

WILDLIFE

Many animals call the mountains of Norway home. Red deer and wild reindeer climb the southern slopes while they watch for the occasional prowling wolf. Wolverines sniff about in search of small animals such as lemmings. Sometimes they find a fallen *elg*, or moose. Many trout and salmon swim in Norway's lakes and rivers. Otters and beavers are also a common sight.

Ocean animals, such as Arctic cod, are an important food source for many Norwegians. Surrounded by northern waters, Svalbard is home to Arctic animals such as polar bears, walruses, and Arctic foxes.

RED DEER

WOLVERINE

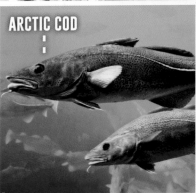
ARCTIC COD

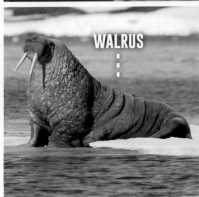
WALRUS

REINDEER

POLAR BEARS

POLAR BEAR

Life Span: **25 to 30 years**
Red List Status: **vulnerable**

polar bear range =

LEAST CONCERN	NEAR THREATENED	VULNERABLE	ENDANGERED	CRITICALLY ENDANGERED	EXTINCT IN THE WILD	EXTINCT
		▲				

11

SAMI PEOPLE

With just over five million people, Norway has a small population compared to its size. Most people have Scandinavian **ancestors**. The majority of the Sami, Norway's **native** group, live in the north. Recently, Norway has received many **immigrants** from Africa and the **Middle East**. About 7 in 10 Norwegians are Lutheran Christians.

Norwegian and Sami are Norway's two national languages. Norwegian has two different systems of writing. *Bokmål*, or "book language," is the most common. *Nynorsk*, or "new Norwegian," is based on the country's many **dialects**.

FAMOUS FACE

Name: Marit Bjørgen
Birthday: March 21, 1980
Hometown: Trondheim, Norway
Famous for: Cross-country skier and the most successful Winter Olympic athlete of all time, winning 15 Olympic medals including 5 medals in the 2018 PyeongChang Olympics and 8 total gold medals

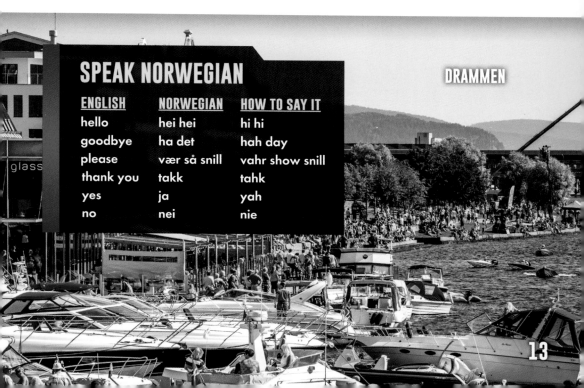

SPEAK NORWEGIAN

ENGLISH	NORWEGIAN	HOW TO SAY IT
hello	hei hei	hi hi
goodbye	ha det	hah day
please	vær så snill	vahr show snill
thank you	takk	tahk
yes	ja	yah
no	nei	nie

DRAMMEN

COMMUNITIES

Four out of every five Norwegians live in cities, which are mostly found in the south or along the western coast. Most of these people live in apartment buildings, though some wealthy Norwegians have single-family homes. **Rural** Norwegians often live in old wooden farmhouses.

BERGEN

SVALBARD

Buses, subways, and bicycles help Norwegians move around in cities. In rural areas, Norwegians often use boats and trains to travel. Cars are also common in the countryside. Snowmobiles are regularly used in northern Norway and Svalbard.

Norwegians are known for being quiet and **reserved**. Equality is important to Norwegians. Many try not to stand out. This is often called *Janteloven*, or "the Law of Jante." It describes the Scandinavian values of putting the community ahead of the individual.

Being outside is important to Norwegians. This is known as *friluftsliv*. Norwegians believe this keeps their bodies and minds strong. Friluftsliv can take many forms, such as outdoor sports, camping trips, or going for bike rides.

THE RIGHT TO ROAM

It is legal to hike and camp almost anywhere in Norway. As long as people respect the land and each other, Norwegians are allowed to explore and enjoy nature.

SCHOOL AND WORK

FOLKEHØGSKOLE

Some Norwegians choose to attend one year of "folk high school." These schools have no exams or grades. They focus on subjects such as music, sports, or theater.

Norwegian children attend school from ages 6 to 16. Students attend three years of secondary school after they complete primary school. They often choose to take three years of upper secondary school afterward. Many Norwegians then continue their education at one of the country's universities.

Most Norwegians have **service jobs** in education, health care, or the government. Others work in **tourism**. Many people who live near the coast work in fishing or the oil industry. A small number of farmers live in the southeastern countryside and mountain valleys.

FARMER

OIL RIG

CROSS-COUNTRY SKIING

Norway is famous for winter sports. Cross-country skiing is the national sport. Norwegians are said to be born with skis on their feet! Ice skating and hockey are also popular in the winter.
In the summer, Norwegians often like to watch and play soccer.

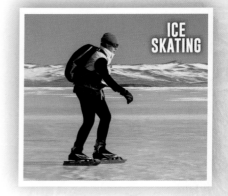

ICE SKATING

Hiking and camping are common in Norway, and the country has thousands of miles of trails. Many families have small cabins in the mountains or on the coast. They like to visit these during the weekend or on holidays.

CAMPING

VIKING RUNES

Write your name using the Viking alphabet!

What You Need:
- rocks
- a pencil
- paint or a permanent marker

Instructions:
1. Find small rocks with at least one flat surface.
2. On the flat surface, use the Viking alphabet to write as much of your name as possible in pencil.
3. Trace the runes with your marker or paints. Then make one for your friends!

Þ	= th	⅄	= æ
ᚠ	= a	Ψ	= z
ᚱ	= r	ᛉ	= s
ᚲ	= k	↑	= t
✕	= g	ᛒ	= b
ᚹ	= w	ᛖ	= e
ᚺ	= h	ᛗ	= m
ᛏ	= n	Γ	= l
ᛁ	= i	◇	= ng
ᛋ	= j	ᛞ	= d
ᛈ	= p	ᛟ	= o

FOOD

PICKING A WINNER

In the summer, many Norwegians search for wild cloudberries. When a patch of cloudberries is found, it is usually kept secret. This allows the same family to pick them again the following year.

EATING CLOUDBERRIES

In Norway, open-faced sandwiches are commonly eaten for breakfast and lunch. These might have a variety of toppings, such as meats, jam, or even herring. Norway's brown goat cheese is regularly eaten as well. Dinners often include meat or fish with potatoes served on the side. Desserts of ice cream or pudding are common.

Waffles and *lefse*, a soft potato flatbread, are favorite snacks. *Fårikål*, a stew with cabbage and mutton, is popular in cold months. Around Christmastime, many families serve *lutefisk*, a special kind of boiled fish.

FÅRIKÅL

LUTEFISK

LEFSE

Norwegians love eating this traditional flatbread for a snack or a dessert. Enjoy it plain or with butter and sugar! Have an adult help you with this recipe.

Ingredients:

5 pounds potatoes, peeled and cut into pieces
1 1/4 cups flour
1/4 cup butter
3 tablespoons heavy cream
1/2 tablespoon salt
1/2 tablespoon sugar

Steps:

1. In a large pot, cover the potatoes with water and cook until tender.

2. Push the potatoes through a potato ricer or a grater into a large bowl.

3. Beat butter, heavy cream, salt, and sugar into the potatoes while they are still warm. Then let the mixture cool to room temperature.

4. Stir flour into the mixture, then pull off pieces of the dough that are about the size of a tablespoon.

5. Lightly flour a pastry cloth or counter. Use a rolling pin to flatten the dough balls into pieces about 1/8 inch (3 millimeters) thick.

6. Heat a griddle to 400 degrees Fahrenheit (204 degrees Celsius), and cook the lefse until bubbles begin forming and each side begins to brown.

7. Let the lefse cool to room temperature, and then enjoy!

Norway's national holiday is Constitution Day on May 17. The day begins with a large breakfast shared with friends and family. Then Norwegians take to the streets. Children parade through the towns, and marching bands play music. People often dress up in a *bunad*, a **traditional** outfit that identifies where someone is from.

On June 23, Norwegians celebrate *Sankt Hans*, or midsummer. This usually includes grilling sausages, lighting bonfires, and staying up late. No matter the time of year, Norwegians love to be outside with friends and family!

CITY SKIING
Every March, Oslo hosts the Holmenkollen Ski Festival. This event brings some of the best cross-country skiers and ski jumpers in the world!

1536
Norway becomes a part of Denmark but still functions independently

AROUND 793
The Viking Age begins

1814
Denmark gives control of Norway to Sweden through a peace treaty, ending their feud during the Napoleonic Wars

AROUND 900
The people of Norway unite into one kingdom

1901
The Nobel Peace Prize is first awarded in Oslo

1030
Christianity comes to Norway

LATE 1960s
Oil and gas are discovered in the North Sea, helping Norway's economy flourish

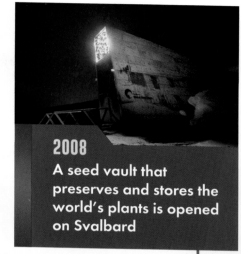

2008
A seed vault that preserves and stores the world's plants is opened on Svalbard

1940
Germany invades Norway during World War II

1905
Norway declares independence from Sweden

1994
The city of Lillehammer hosts the Winter Olympics

Official Name: Kingdom of Norway

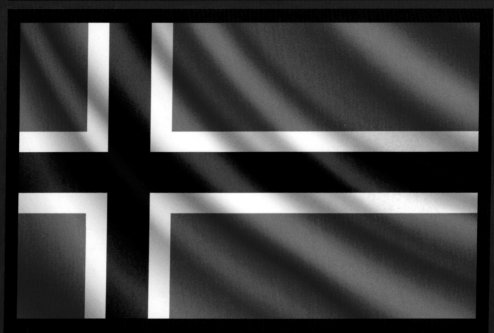

Flag of Norway: The Norwegian flag is red with a blue cross outlined in white. This flag design is known as the Nordic cross, and Norway shares it with Denmark, Finland, Iceland, and Sweden. The colors red and white represent past connections to Denmark, and blue is for past connections to Sweden.

Area: 125,021 square miles
(323,802 square kilometers)

Capital City: Oslo

Important Cities: Bergen, Stavanger, Trondheim

Population:
5,372,191 (July 2018)

COUNTRYSIDE
17.8%

WHERE
PEOPLE LIVE

CITY
82.2%

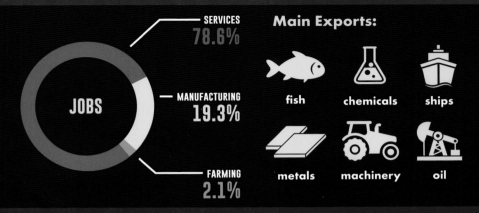

JOBS

SERVICES
78.6%

MANUFACTURING
19.3%

FARMING
2.1%

Main Exports:

fish

chemicals

ships

metals

machinery

oil

National Holiday:
Constitution Day, May 17

Main Languages:
Norwegian and Sami

Form of Government:
parliamentary constitutional monarchy

Title for Country Leaders:
prime minister (head of government),
king (chief of state)

RELIGION

LUTHERAN
70.6%

OTHER
CHRISTIAN
6.7%

OTHER
19.5%

MUSLIM
3.2%

Unit of Money:
Norwegian krone

GLOSSARY

ancestors—relatives who lived long ago

Arctic Circle—an imaginary line that circles the top of the globe, parallel to the equator

dialects—local ways of speaking particular languages

fjords—long, deep inlets of a sea that are lined by mountains

funicular—related to a railway that uses a cable and balanced cars to go up and down a mountainside

glaciers—massive sheets of ice that cover large areas of land

Gulf Stream—a strong ocean current that brings warm water from the Gulf of Mexico across the Atlantic Ocean

immigrants—people who move to a new country

mainland—the main part of a country that is usually connected to a larger continent

Middle East—a region of southwestern Asia and northern Africa; this region includes Egypt, Lebanon, Iran, Iraq, Israel, Saudi Arabia, Syria, and other nearby countries.

native—originally from the area or related to a group of people that began in the area

peninsula—a section of land that extends out from a larger piece of land and is almost completely surrounded by water

plateaus—areas of flat, raised land

reserved—cautious in words and actions

rural—related to the countryside

Scandinavia—a region of northern Europe that includes Sweden, Denmark, and Norway

service jobs—jobs that perform tasks for people or businesses

terrain—the surface features of an area of land

tourism—the business of people traveling to visit other places

traditional—related to customs, ideas, or beliefs handed down from one generation to the next

TO LEARN MORE

AT THE LIBRARY

Kagda, Sakina. *Norway*. New York, N.Y.: Cavendish Square Publishing, 2017.

Leaf, Christina. *Denmark*. Minneapolis, Minn.: Bellwether Media, 2020.

Mara, Wil. *Norway*. New York, N.Y.: Children's Press, 2017.

ON THE WEB

FACTSURFER

Factsurfer.com gives you a safe, fun way to find more information.

1. Go to www.factsurfer.com.

2. Enter "Norway" into the search box and click 🔍.

3. Select your book cover to see a list of related web sites.

INDEX

The images in this book are reproduced through the courtesy of: Christina Leaf, front cover; Nokuro pp. 4-5; Andrey Armyago, p. 5 (Geirangerfjord); Hroch, p. 5 (Jotunheimen National Park); Viktor Hladchenko, p. 5 (Kjerag); Popova Valeriya, p. 5 (Oslo Opera House); ginger_polina_bublik, p. 8; Morten Normann Almeland, p. 9 (top); Ihor Kontsurov, p. 9 (bottom); MarcinWojc, p. 10 (reindeer); Ondrej Prosicky, p. 10 (red deer); Alexandr Junek Inaging, p. 10 (wolverine); Valentina Photo, p. 10 (arctic cod); Inge Jansen, p. 10 (walrus); Himanshi Saraf, pp. 10-11; age fotostock / Alamy Stock Photo, p. 12; dpa picture alliance archive / Alamy Stock Photo, p. 13 (top); BAAS, p. 13 (bottom); aaabbbccc, p. 14; Alexander Lutsenko / Alamy Stock Photo, p. 15; Dmitry Naumov, p. 16; Pere Sanz / Alamy Stock Photo, p. 17; Anders Ryman / Alamy Stock Photo, p. 18; Steve Heap, p. 19 (top); V. Belov, p. 19 (bottom); Espen E, p. 20 (top); ivandan, p. 20 (bottom); Anastasiia Shavshyna, p. 21; Jouni Tormanen / Alamy Stock Photo, p. 22; StockphotoVideo, p. 23 (top); Fanfo, p. 23 (middle); Julie Vader, p. 23 (bottom); Kjersti Joergensen, p. 24; Ragnar Singsaas / Contributor, p. 25; Zimneva Natalia, p. 26; ginger_polina_bublik, p. 27 (top); INTERFOTO / Alamy Stock Photo, p. 27 (bottom); Anton Ivanov / Alamy Stock Photo, p. 29 (bill); Bragin Alexey, p. 29 (coin).